Sales Tales

By Kent David

The Truth is "The answer is always no, if you don't ask",

and I will show you how to ask in a natural way so that it is part of the conversation and the sale.

Acknowledgements

This book would not be possible without the support of my favorite people. My wife, Guqueta and my daughters Keegan and Morgan. I love them very much and I am thankful for their support and encouragement. Their critiques kept me on track and their prodding kept me moving forward.

Introduction

Hello and welcome to Sales Tales. You've taken a great step forward into polishing your sales skills by reading these short sales tales. You will be amazed at how these short sales tales will demonstrate a selling skill that you will then pick up and be able to use as your own. These short sales tales are entertaining, fun and educational. The suggestion, is to read one story, put the book down, think of your own life and find a similar story that has a similar point and is familiar. That way the sales skill will become ingrained in you because it will be natural to you and truthful. Then when you are in a sales situation and the right opportunity presents itself, your mind will automatically trigger the sales method for you to use because it will be a situation that you are already familiar with.

Best Wishes and Good Selling

Table of Contents

Rule of Reciprocation and Gift Giving

Are You Listening or Just Hearing?

Favors

Tidbit #1 Buyer's Remorse

Please Call Me Back

Harper

When You Coming Home Dad

Tidbit #2 Gift of Gab

What's In It For Me

So What

Milk

Tidbit #3 Their IQ is Higher than Their Credit Score

Jimmy and the Grill

Nothing Sells Itself

No Humor

Family Court

Tidbit #4 Manipulation versus Selling

Senior Discount

Only One Can Speak

I Missed It

Rule of Reciprocation and Gift Giving

As I drove into the parking lot I could see the bright red firetruck by the front doors of the local Walmart and my first thought was oh-oh, what's going on. Then I saw the fireman standing around the truck with their boots held high in the air, waving, asking for donations. Mostly being ignored by incoming customers but getting some donations. My thought was, where do I park so that I can go in, get the milk I need and not be bothered by another donation seeker. I had already been hit on twice this week and another donation seeker just seemed tiring. One of those occasions where you just try to get by them by not making eye contact because you have already been hit on for donations the last two times you went to the store to get bread and sandwich meat. You're prepared to say to them, I'll catch you on the way out, but not really mean it. I made it. No one accosted me and I was now inside the giant Walmart grabbing a buggy. I gathered everything on my shopping list and headed out the other exit, trying again to avoid the fundraising pack.

And there she was, just inside the exit doors of the giant Walmart standing next to her mom. The cutest little girl that you have ever seen, you know the ones. The one with hair curls flowing down her back, dressed in her best Sunday dress with white socks and shoes that showed her mother had spent a lot to time to dress her so pretty and a neatly tied bow in her hair that said, "I'm a little angel, look at my innocent smile. Her smile showed that she was missing her two front teeth, but it didn't matter. It was a smile she shared with everyone and it lit up her face. It was a smile that spread from ear to ear. She held a small blue plastic bowl that matched her dress, and was full of peel off stickers. They were Fireman stickers that showed support for the Bryant Fire department. She held out a sticker towards me and said with a lisp in her soft voice, "you want a sticker"? She was obviously someone who liked stickers. She had several on her dress and arms. She even had one on her rosy cheek. I said sure and took the sticker from her. Her voice then seemed to lower several octaves and she said, "That will be a dollar". I was stunned, and said oh, ok and reached in my pocket for a dollar. After she pocketed her sale, she looked at me again and her voice returned to that soft sweet angelic voice of before as she said, "you want another one"? This time I was prepared. I said no thanks and headed out to the amateur fireman fundraisers outside. I had just been sold by a five year old using the sales technique 'Rule of reciprocation and gift giving'.

The Rule of Reciprocation and Gift Giving

We feel obligated to repay a favor, gift or invitation when we receive them with something of equal value. The gift or favor does not have to be requested to be obligatory. Simply accepting the gift obligates you subconsciously. As a salesperson we can use this rule to engage a customer. When you are approaching a customer, offering to take them to lunch, or offering them a free hat or ink pen, subconsciously obligates them to further contact where the sale can begin. It is a strong technique to engage the customer. As I left the store thinking about what had just happened, I looked over my shoulder to hear her engage the next customer she had zeroed in on. She probably raised more money that day than all the fireman put together.

I smiled and decided to wear the sticker.

Are you Listening or just Hearing?

My wife and I went to look for a new car. They were all clean and shiny, not at all like the one we were driving with the four year-old french fry stuck down between the seats. Far enough down that I couldn't reach it with my hand but still there after several attempts at vacuuming it loose. My daughter had thrown it to me in a game of share with daddy when she was two. The car lot was like a circus, cars were everywhere, cars with balloons on the antennas, cars under a carnival tent and one was even spinning in a circle in the center of it all. There was barely room for us to park our dull dirty rust bucket of a vehicle. The one spinning in a circle was a two seater blue Fiat Spider convertible and even though I knew it wasn't the family car we had come to look at, we walked over to look at the price and features on the sticker. We had owned one when we were first married and I was selling vacuum cleaners door to door. I was curious about what had changed on the car and for a moment, I was remembering my younger days. I saw in my mind's eye, my wife and I driving scenic highway 1 along the California coast line, inches from the cliffs edge, with the top down and the salty sea air blowing in all around us. A gorgeous blue sky and a view of the ocean that is priceless. Rod Stewarts song "Maggie May" was blaring on the speakers. Everyone looks; it doesn't necessarily mean you're in the market to buy, sometimes it is just nostalgia. I am a responsible adult now and I think to myself, when did that sneak up on me? When we were first married, we would use my paycheck to pay the bills and use my wife's to spend on anything and everything with nothing to show for it by the following Monday. I think I know the moment I became a responsible grownup. It was when my first daughter was born and my wife placed her in my arms, looked at me and said "what do we do now"? I now look at ice cream in the grocery store but my waist line tells me to go look at the salads. I buy life insurance, mow the yard and I have cleaned up baby vomit. For the sake of my stomach, we won't even mention some of the other things I had to clean up. I was back to reality by the time the salesman rushed out to introduce himself. I told him that we had come in to look at, a family sedan. He asked if I wanted to test drive this hot car spinning in the center and I said no, we were looking for a family car. I had a wife, two kids, a dog and all the kids' friends and sports equipment we needed to haul around each weekend so we needed a family car. I don't think he heard me because he repeated that I should test drive this hot rod. I thought, maybe he didn't hear me so I repeated again that we weren't interested and he motioned for his manager to come over. I thought good, now we will get somewhere, we'll have somebody who can hear. I restated our need again, that we were looking for a family car and I thought he was listening, he shook my hand, was looking me in the eye, but then he spoke. The first words out of his mouth after the introductions were, "do me a favor and just test drive this baby"! I paused; what, didn't you hear me I laughed in my head. They had both asked a favor and both knew the social rule of favors but were applying it poorly because they weren't listening. My wife and I were friendly to them but we were not friends. They heard me but they didn't understand. We were both speaking the same language but our understanding of each other was totally absent. It's just like when you go through the drive through at the fast food restaurant, that is where the French fry came from, but the speaker system has so much static that you can't understand what they are asking and you don't know if they understand what you are saying. We probably could have gotten further in the conversation if I had just resorted back to my toddler days and pointed at the parking lot, made a motion like turning a steering wheel and said bye-bye. Their goal was to put me inside that vehicle because that's what they had been taught by management. Nothing else mattered. Not my needs, not my wants, just what they wanted to sell. Put the customer behind the wheel and the car will sell itself was their thinking, not the mindset of what does the customer want or need and then addressing that. They were both trying to sell what they wanted to sell, not what I wanted to buy. They were the ones sold on that spinning relic of the past, I needed a family sedan and I was getting irritated. What made it frustrating for me as a customer was that I told them my wants and needs upfront, they did not have to use any special skills to uncover my wants or needs and they didn't have to help me learn what I wanted or needed by using careful questioning, they simply needed to listen. After their third insistence my wife and I just dropped our chins, sighed and left. Sometimes it's just hard to buy.

There is a simple way of learning to listen. Repeating what the customer says is their need or summarizing what the customer has stated as their need can help the salesperson clarify and firm up the need with the customer. Don't be like a parrot by repeating everything, but asking to clarify what the customer means when they say "I am interested in a hot water recirculation pump", can help the salesperson as well as the customer nail down the need. Simply ask, "I want to make sure I understand that what you need is a pump that recirculates hot water"? This does two things, one it tells the customer that you are listening and two that it is important to you. If you want to become an expert at the skill of listening, pull out a pocket notepad and when the customer tells you what they want, write it down as you repeat it. This will replace your hearing with listening. Your ears are required to hear, your mind is required to listen and write. You don't have to get it 100% right, just close enough for the customer to either agree that you are correct or clear up any misunderstanding you might have. If they haven't already told you, why do they need a hot water recirculating pump? What are they trying to accomplish? Why is that important? Any of those clarifying questions will help you have a clear idea of what the customer wants to buy and will help you interpret your understanding into how your product can help fulfill the want or need. Salespeople should understand that people don't necessarily want a drill, they want the hole. The drill is just the solution to get the hole and they may not need a drill at all, maybe the solution is for a hole punch that you sell. The point is, listening will help the salesperson uncover and clarify the need. You will then be able to help the customer get to the right solution for their need and your sales will go up. The car salesmen had unintentionally built an invisible roadblock so the sale couldn't begin. The car salespeople had lost the opportunity to help us buy because of their lack of listening skill and lost opportunities are one of the things that separate the great sales earners from the average.

I turn on the radio as I drive off the lot and guess who's song is playing.

Favors

My brother in law, Ace is a great fisherman. He grew up in the "Holler" hunting and fishing for dinner. He claims he could put a bucket of water in the backyard and then go out the next day, fish in that bucket, and catch all the fish you could eat. He is not far from being truthful. He routinely has his freezers full of fish and wild game, but he is not great on sharing his bounty with extended family members. Let's just say sharing is not his strong suit. Maybe every year or two, he will need to clean out his freezers of food that his family hasn't eaten and offer to share that with those of us who are hunter gatherer challenged. The other day he came over to ask a favor for help in filling out insurance papers and I thought, boy it would be great weekend to have one of his famous catfish cookouts. It had been a couple of years at least since the last one. He has a large deep fryer attached to a 20lb propane tank with four burners. It sounds like a jet engine when he lights it. The fish cooker uses 2 gallons of cooking oil. His homemade fryer travels with him to the deer woods in the winter and when he is cooking, you can smell the food from the main road as you get close to the camp. It is so big that he has to use his truck just to move it. Ace has this down to a science. He coats the fish in his secret cornbread mix, using a filet sifter that puts just the right amount of his secret cornbread mix on the fish. He fills the fish fryer with fresh peanut oil that he brings to a boil, and when the temperature is just right, he drops in catfish filets that come out golden brown and mouthwatering. He always adds french fries and hush puppy's to round out the cookout. Good is not a sufficient word to describe this feast. As we were sealing the envelopes to mail the insurance paperwork, I put a stamp on the envelopes and looked at Ace and jokingly said, "this was an expensive favor he had asked of me, referring to the postage stamps I had provided. The insurance forms were complicated and took us quite a while to complete them. I told him my daughter and her boyfriend were coming in this weekend to visit, and this would be a great time for a fish cookout, do you have any fish?" Ace smiled broadly and proudly announced that he did indeed have freezers that needed to be thinned out and agreed that he would fry up some of his fish. It would be a good weekend to have a fish cookout, the weather was predicted to be sunny and in the mid-seventies. I could already taste the fish. When you ask a favor of someone, you are more positively received if you give a reason for the favor and when I told Ace that my daughter was coming in from out of town, the reason for my request was understandable to Ace in a family and social way. Favors are generally reserved for friends. Favors obligate the customer but they also obligate the salesperson. They have to be repaid with something of equal or more value. As Charles de Montesquieu said "a favor is an arrangement between parties in an attempt to exchange a small favor for a bigger one." We feel obligated to repay the favor and the favor does not have to be requested to be effective at invoking the social rule of favors. As the salesperson, when you are asked for a favor, respond to the customer and close the sale by saying, "if I can do this Abc thing you're asking, can we agree to move forward with Xyz? If as a salesperson you are asking a favor of the customer, "give a reason for the customer to agree to the favor request. Would you Mr. Customer do me a favor of meeting earlier at say, 3pm? I have a dentist appointment at 4:30. If you are the customer trying to get the sales clerk to honor the sale price that went off yesterday or you're trying to get them to give you a better room at the hotel you're staying in, try this. Start by saying it exactly like this "I know you would help me if you could, is it possible for you to ____ , I need to ____" . This does a couple of things. One it requests a favor and gives a reason for asking; two it invokes the "I can" from the person you are asking because it empowers them to take ownership of the decision. We all want to believe that there is nothing we can't do in our world when the decisions regarding yes or no are ours to make. There is another side to the use of favors. A negative side. If used incorrectly, like in the story "Are you listening or just hearing", a request for a favor can destroy the sale and sour the sales relationship before the sale can begin. Use the social rule of favors carefully and you will enjoy an enhanced sales interaction that is productive for the customer who wants to buy and for you the salesperson who has something to offer, whether it is a product, service, or intangible action. I can hardly wait for some hot golden brown catfish filets. Let's eat.

Tidbit #1

Buyer's Remorse

My wife say's "I'm feeling pretty good about you right now, don't push it"! She is referring to my behavior regarding the dinner and theater I took her to but she is cautioning me.

I had asked her out, taken her to her favorite restaurant and then to the theater. I am fishing for compliments about how good I am. I want compliments about how great I did in planning the evening and all the hard work I went to in order to make a memorable evening for her. I am not satisfied with what I think are her mediocre appreciative compliments, so I reiterate all the effort that went into this special evening just for her. Okay, maybe I am acting a little immature but I still fish for more. I want her to say it was the greatest evening of her life and the best compliment she can come up is like the last time I cooked dinner. She said "I ate it". Not a great compliment in my opinion.

I go over the trouble I went to again and how lucky she is to be married to someone so romantic. She has never been one to heap on the praise but she has just reminded me. Don't oversell it. After you have closed the sale, reaffirm the customers purchase by telling them that they have made the correct decision and you will successfully minimize any buyer's remorse, but going back through the selling features and benefits can actually un-sell what you have just accomplished. It creates unease, irritation, regret and possibly buyer's remorse.

I like being married to her. I shut up.

Please Call Me Back

My mother in law is old. Her body may be elderly, but her mind is as sharp and young as ever. She also is sometimes a smart aleck. I think my wife got her razor sarcastic wit from her. She was sitting in her living room and someone called from an eight hundred number she didn't recognize but she instantly knew it was probably a telemarketer; she doesn't have any friends with an eight hundred number. She picked up the phone and said hello and the computer on the other end started connecting her to a live person, unbeknownst to them, she had a second call ringing in from another eight hundred number that she didn't recognize. She asked the person on the first call to hold on for just a second while she answered that call because she thought it was her son or daughter. She then told that telemarketer she was going to conference them into the call she was on with her daughter so they could explain everything because she was old and didn't want to miss anything. She conferenced them in to the first number. Now she had two telemarketers on the same phone call, each thinking they are talking to the daughter of this elderly woman. She started acting like she was confused and wanted them to start over and explain why they were calling to the other one. She sat the phone down and continued knitting her sweater. I guess the confusion on the line was too much for the telemarketers and eventually they hung up the line. She doesn't like robo calls and caller i.d. has changed telemarketing the way that scam artists and con men have stopped people from opening their doors to strangers. It can be a struggle to actively go after new customers in the age when people won't open answer the door to strangers for fear of a criminal wanting to commit a home invasion. People don't answer the phone from numbers they don't recognize, but human curiosity is an amazing thing. We are not only creatures of habit, we are curious about everything. A cave man salesperson went from cave to cave looking for customers who needed fire on demand but it was time consuming and he was on the trail constantly. Fast forward to today. The phone has been invented so we could connect with each other but so many companies have abused the phone for contact, telemarketing is dramatically less effective than it once was. There is a way to use the phone more effectively as a telemarketing tool. Let's say for example you are salesperson calling on a company and you can't reach the decision makers to see if they would have a need for your product. You have tried to get an appointment but for whatever reason it just isn't happening. Maybe you have talked to several people at the company and they all are referring you to someone else as the person you need to speak to but you can't get in contact with them. You call people but they don't take or return your calls. Is there a way to get someone you haven't interacted with to call you back, most of the time if not every time? Yes, and it is easy. Ninety percent of the people will return your call with this technique when used properly.

A lot of busy business people will let their phone calls roll over to voicemail, especially for numbers they don't recognize so they aren't bothered by telemarketers and others they see as a waste of their time. That is great because that is what works in our favor. This technique can only be used once on each person and you do need to be able and willing to answer the return call. You must not let your phone go to voicemail. Here is how it works. Call the persons number you are trying to reach and when you get their voicemail, say exactly this, exactly this way, "Hello, My name is (insert your name) my number is (insert your phone number). I am calling in reference to….. (hang up at this instant leaving the voicemail incomplete). Now be prepared with what you will say when they call you back because the majority of people will return the call. Practice this twenty times before you actually use it for real because missed opportunities are what separate the average sales earner from the above average and you can only use this technique once for each new contact. Use it twice at your own peril, they will instantly see this as manipulation and the sales opportunity will be lost. My mother in law is still knitting the sweater that has turned into a blanket. You can call her but be wary if she wants to conference you in to an existing call.

Harper

Harper is a talkative constant motion three year old. She has a smile for everyone and will talk your ear off. When she was two, you might not be able to understand a word of what she was saying but she would talk, if you were willing to listen. She can sure tell a story. She brushes the hair from her face and in an excited voice she will spin you a tale of adventure. If you don't laugh at the parts she thinks you should, she will. Saying, she will tell you a story is a misnomer, it is an epic, complete with waving arms, clapped hands and laughter. There is a lot of joy in her voice. Her grandfather, Rocky, is my brother in law and Rocky has bought a puppy for Harper. She loves playing with the puppy. Gail is irritated though. Gail is Rocky's wife and she has reason to be upset with Rocky. He bought this puppy for Harper without discussing it with her. The puppy has been getting out of the backyard fence and running around loose in the yard. Gail is worried that the puppy will get lost or accidently hurt. She is adamant that he get to the bottom of the method of the puppy escapes and put a stop to it. She keeps telling Rocky that the dog is in danger of being run over because the road in front of their house is a very busy road and traffic is zooming by. She is also reiterating for the third time that the puppy could be hurt by some other danger that she won't clarify. She is miffed, and the look she gives Rocky is a "do this" or else. I won't be happy with you until you figure it out. Since this is the fifth time today the puppy has gotten out of the fenced area of the back yard, it is also the fifth time today that Gail has reminded him that it is his responsibility to fix the problem. He had bought the puppy so it is his responsibility. He decides the better course of action than playing with Harper, is to look for how the puppy is getting out. The whole happy wife, happy life saying is flashing in Rocky's mind. For the rest of the day he searches for the puppy's escape path. Rocky has surveyed the fence for any weak spots where the puppy can escape but he is frustrated because he can't find the spot. He has walked around the fence multiple times and even tried to look at the fence from a puppy's viewpoint by getting down on all fours and scouring the fence for weak points. He has tried to think like a puppy, from both the inside and outside views. The fence looks secure, it is down to the ground and there are no gaps at all that he can find. He just can't figure it out. He is puzzled. The puppy has the upper hand and meanwhile Gail is insisting he put a stop to the escapes because every time she looks out the window of her kitchen, the puppy is out of the fenced part of the yard and is running loose. Gail is yelling at Rocky that the puppy is out again so my brother in law goes out once again to put the puppy back inside the backyard fence. He has been out all day trying to solve the mystery. How is this happening? The puppy seems to be an escape artist extraordinaire. Finally, after another futile search, Rocky is standing next to the fence with Harper by his side and as they are both looking at the fence, he asks her if she knows how the puppy is getting out of the fence. Harper simply replies "yes". Rocky says "can you show Grandpa where the puppy is getting out"? Harper walks over to the gate and grabs the gate latch and says "I open gate, and puppy come out". Why is it that we make things harder than they have to be. Two simple questions and the problem was solved. My brother in law spent hours upon hours trying to figure out how the puppy was escaping but in the end, all he had to do was ask the customer. Sometimes it's that way in selling. Asking the customer, the right question, can get us to the best solution that is needed to solve the customer's problem. There is a method of problem solving that was created in the twelfth century and is attributed to an English Franciscan Friar named William Ockham (c.1287-1347). The principle named after Ockham is called Occam's razor. The essence of the method is; When faced with competing solutions, the one with the fewest assumptions is likely to be the correct solution. Going to the person (customer) who benefited from the purchase of the puppy and asking them if they knew how the puppy was getting out, provided the solution. The same can be said for your customers. Ask them, when there is a problem, if they know how the problem happened, you may find that the customer doesn't fully understand the products use and who knows, they may be opening the gate. Woof! Woof!

When You Coming Home Dad

My daughter has a play tonight at school but I have already explained to her that I am going to be out of town and will miss her starring role. She has been practicing for several weeks and from the scenes I saw in my living room, she will be quite good. I explain that I wish I could be there, but this trip is important, and I can't miss work, I tell her that I hope she understands, and she says she does, but I see the downturned smile and the look on her face has a little expression of disappointment. I leave for work thinking, what cheap manipulation with the sad face and even though I smile at her attempt, I won't be swayed by something so childish; I have business to take care of. Sometimes daughters use manipulation to get what they want from dear old dad but sometimes, dad is a hard case. The customer I am going to see is important and since they are a long ways away, I will be traveling overnight and can't make the play. There will be another play I tell myself. About lunch time I notice that I have a voicemail. When I check it, it is my daughter singing a song, "Cat's in the Cradle", a 1974 folk rock song by Harry Chapin from his album Verities & Balderdash. That's all, no comment about my missing her play, no mention of anything of any kind, just the first verse of the song. "my child arrived just the other day, he came to the world in the usual way, but there were planes to catch and bills to pay, he learned to walk while I was away". Later that night while I am sitting in the audience watching my daughter debut in her school play, I smile and think, she is very skilled at manipulation; I sarcastically admit, she gets it from her mother. My twelve-year-old daughter has perfected her use of the 'back the hearse up and let 'em smell the roses' sales technique. If you're not familiar with it, I highly encourage you to learn it. Depending on the situation, it can be an effective technique at moving the sale forward but is a manipulative and adversarial close so use it only as a last resort. It should be in your sales toolbox but it has been regulated to the negative history of long ago sales techniques. It typically was used by insurance salesmen and is responsible for some of society's negative ideas about salespeople. I recently saw an ad from a life insurance company using a version of it to ask, "what will happen to your family if something happens to you".

Learn it; perfect it; just don't teach it to your daughters.

Tidbit #2 Gift of Gab

I have heard people describe a quality in salespeople as he/she has the "gift of gab". Sometimes it's a compliment on the smoothness in a salespersons presentation or their ability to close the sale, but sometimes it isn't a compliment; meaning they never shut up. One of the key training components of your sales training should be a measure of how much you talk versus how much the customer talks. If you are talking more than half the time, then the customer is probably getting short changed because you are not reaching the full understanding of the customers wants and needs. If you are talking less than half the time, then you are probably in a selling mode. So how do you know? Think about it and honestly judge yourself. Are you a Chatty Cathy or a Silent Sam?

What's In It For Me

Do you have a favorite Girl Scout cookie? Mine are the thin mints but I haven't tasted one yet that I didn't like. They only come around once a year so I stock up. I am also a sucker for kids selling things. My oldest daughter was in girl scouts. She sold cookies, calendars, hair bows and who knows what else. It seems that their troop was mostly about selling things and raising money. She had just completed a successful season selling cookies and her troop was setting up in front of Walmart to sell what remained of the undelivered cookies. Some customers signed up to purchase cookies but when it came time to pay, they were nowhere to be found. My daughter was always thinking of ways to enhance the system to her benefit and was setting outside the grocery store pushing the thin mints, She was explaining to the customer about how good they were and that they were awesome. As I walked up to the table, I overheard her tell them that the cookies were three dollars a box. At that time they were two fifty so this three dollar quote my daughter was saying, immediately sent off alarms. After questioning her for a little bit, we discovered she had indeed been selling boxes of cookies for three dollars. We asked why she was charging more than the regular asking price and she said "if I sell them for $2.50, then what's in it for me? We explained the idea of volunteerism for the greater good but that ended her career selling Girl Scout cookies; we couldn't allow her to continue selling the cookies, but she had made a good point. The customer just like the salesperson always silently asks "what's in it for me". When we give the customer an offer, we should be ready and able to answer the question that the customer is asking in their head "what is in it for me", the customer. My daughter saw that she was doing all the work while the Girl Scout leader had all the money. She never saw the benefit of her effort and wanted something for herself to compensate for it. She had been selling cookies, calendars and pencils to long. She refunded the person I had heard her talk to, and I don't think she had spoken too many, but we wouldn't let her sell cookies anymore. She's not dishonest, quite the contrary, she is a hard worker and a studious student. My daughter has a good heart but what is the Russian adage; Trust, but Verify. She just wants to be rewarded for what she does and is not ashamed to admit it. She also has great character. She is the one in the family that we all say has broken wing syndrome. You know the one, the one that finds a bird with a broken wing, takes it in, feeds it, cares for it, nurses it back to health and when the bird pecks you and flies off, she cries sadly for a while but in the end is happy. Later in her school years she brought home a foreign exchange student that was being neglected in her host home. The exchange student was scared to stay with the host family, not of the family, but of the environment she had been placed in. Imagine being in a foreign country, not speaking the language well, and living way back in the woods in a rundown mobile home trailer. When the host family goes off to deer camp, leaving the foreign exchange student by themselves, they take the only heater in the house with them. The host family should never have been allowed to host a foreign exchange student, but I don't want to get on that soapbox right now. The student ended up staying at our house for the most of the rest of the year and became a dear family friend. Back to the story about my daughter. Her troop sold calendars one year and I showed my daughter the rule of concession and she ran with it. She would go door to door in her Girl Scout uniform and ask the homeowner if they wanted to buy a calendar for a dollar; if they said no, she would concede and say ok, how about a pencil for twenty five cents. She sold a lot of calendars and a lot of pencils. We had to put a stop to that also because her troop was making money hand over fist but we thought it was getting out of hand and wanted her to focus on schoolwork not fundraising. My daughter hadn't done anything wrong in selling the cookies for three dollars; she had simply as a child, expressed the rule of self-interest. The rule of self-interest is that people want to get the most and pay the least for their choice and they always ask "what's in it for me"? You can call it value, the customer does; and the salesperson should, but understanding that the customer needs to see the benefit of the product as it applies to them, not just the feature, demonstrates to them the value. When you are consistent with the rule of self-interest, you will be more likely to complete the sale, when you don't, you won't.

We all want to know, "what's in it for me?"

So What

Hard to believe but my youngest daughter was starting college. It wouldn't be long and she would be living on her own. I asked her one time that spring what she thought it would take to live on her own and she said about $500 a month. Rent, food, utilities, gas, the whole ball of wax. At that time the cost of rent alone ran about $750 a month. We laughed because she wasn't privy to the cost of life while growing up, so we joked that we wished for those days of a kid's inexperience. She wanted to go east to college, one of the big-name schools like Duke, with a big price tag to match but that wasn't in our budget, so she would be going to the local university. We told her it wasn't important where she got her degree but what she got her degree in and what she did with it that was important. We had planned on her driving my old truck the kids affectionately called hubba dubba to school but it was on its last legs. My wife and I talked about it and I really didn't trust hubba-dubba to take her safely back and forth so it was time to get her a car. Something that was cheap like me and like me, reliable. The first car we looked at was a Chevrolet cavalier. Like hubba-dubba, I thought it had also seen better days but she saw flashy cute. It was purple. She always was the kid that liked pink and green polka dot dresses and colorful self-expressive outfits. I resisted buying this car and thank goodness the salesperson made it easy by being unskilled at his profession in selling. He fumbled along with her and that helped me by his unknowingly putting up roadblocks to the sale. The salesperson helped her be the one to decide that this purple lemon was not for her and we left the lot. After searching for a few months we came to the conclusion that it was going to be difficult to find a good reliable used car. She came up with a plan. If she could secure enough scholarships to pay for tuition, would we buy her a NEW car? We said yes, what kind of car was she talking about? I knew the estimated cost of four years of college tuition so we set that as our price point for looking at which car she could look for. That spring she searched high and low for scholarships. The hunt was on. There aren't a lot of scholarships for middle class, second generation, young ladies but wow, did she apply for everything. I think she even applied for a scholarship for people with brown curly hair. She was successful in getting enough for a semester's tuition. She closed the sale. I had agreed to her terms and she had done her part in getting the first semester paid for. What would happen the rest of the four years really didn't matter, she was trying. I asked her what car she had picked out and she said there were two that she Loved. One was a Mazda Tribute and the other was a Nissan Xterra. We went to look at both. While looking at the Nissan, she was leaning into the back seat on one side of the car and I was leaning in from the other side. The salesman was in the front leaning over the front seats pointing out the features of the car. He began to explain the child safety restraints and went into great detail about how it had three points of contact, parachute rip cord restraints; universal swivel buckles and so on, and so on. My daughter looked up at me and in a pause in the sales description she said "that's great, but I don't even have a boyfriend. When we left the dealership she asked me why the salesperson was talking so much about stuff she couldn't care less about and never once asked her what she was looking for in a car or why. I explained that most salespeople throw up as much stuff into the conversation as they can to see what sticks. They don't think to stop and ask what are you looking for? At the Mazda dealership, the salesperson said "wow, going off to college is exciting. Look at all the room this car has to haul your stuff". The salesperson may have gotten lucky, but it was a relevant point to her. Making a point that is relevant to the customers wants or needs, moves the sale forward and conversely, not making your point relevant, just adds static to the conversation and puts another roadblock up to the sale. You don't have to rely on luck to hit a relevant point. Ask yourself before you talk about a feature or benefit of the product you are representing; "So What". If you can answer "so what" the way your customer will answer, then you are moving the sale forward. If you can't answer "so what" the way your customer will, don't make the point, it's not relevant. Make it a habit by trying it when you buy something today. Look at the feature and ask "so what", this will become a second nature habit if you practice.

Milk

Asking someone to do something or to use a product and assuming that they know all the intricacies on exactly how you want them to do it, even something as simple as drinking milk, can result in utter failure and chaos. Customers don't always know how to use your product. The directions aren't always clear. Sometimes the owner's manual is missing. We were at a family get together and my daughter was asked to get something to drink for the toddler sitting in the middle of the living room floor. My daughter is nine years old and graciously accepts the task. She gets up, goes to the kitchen and pours a glass of milk. She comes back to the living room and hands the glass to the baby who quickly upends the glass and is drenched in a full glass of milk. Milk is everywhere, the baby is soaked, the floor looks like the great flood has just happened. Now everyone is looking at my daughter and asking, "What were you thinking"? Other women are jumping into action with paper towels and scowls. Why would someone give a full glass of something to drink to a baby when the baby doesn't even know how to drink from a cup? Not a sippie cup, a full blown twelve ounce glass sized beverage. The point is this; just because you know how to do something doesn't mean everyone else does, so take the time to carefully explain how to do what you are asking them to do and if you're unsure they know how to use your product, take the time to show them how to use it properly. Why? You will have fewer returns, a happier customer experience and less chaos in your sales day. Anyone have cookies to go with that milk?

Tidbit #3 Their IQ is higher than Their Credit Score

Sometimes the customer has little, none or just plain bad credit. The question you have to answer is; do you really want the sale from someone who, by their own credit history, will not pay you? The time it takes to manage an account like that might be better spent pursuing more reliable and profitable payers.

Jimmy and the Grill

Sometimes unforeseen forces can dramatically affect your performance and the outcome of the sale. My son in law, "Jimmy" likes meat. He will forgo the veggies and zero in on a good hamburger or roast like it is his job. He is a carnivore at his core. His cholesterol is a problem. He comes from the Midwest part of the country and grilling was a common activity for family gatherings. His family would have cook outs around a traditional charcoal grill and Jimmy would salivate while the bratwurst roasted. He believes the best bar-b-que is a charcoal grill that could double as a blacksmiths furnace, capable of smelting iron billets into swords, and he uses the intense heat to sear the steaks into glistening and appetizing feasts. He can cook but he is also mechanically challenged. My daughter says he couldn't put the grill together if it only had one piece. It's a recipe for disaster. After they married, they moved to Kansas for her new job. Jimmy decided that it was time for a cook out and went to the local big box store for a grill. He bought the grill, charcoal, lighter fluid and steaks. Bringing it all home and assembling the grill was a challenge but they did get it ready for the cookout. He piled on the charcoal, loaded it down with lots of lighter fluid and lit the match. What he had not foreseen was the Kansas wind. In Kansas, you have miles and miles of wind mills producing electricity. They are everywhere. It's because the wind in Kansas blows hard and blows constantly and it's a great state for electricity generation via the wind. The wind can also be destructive. In this instance, it blew the roaring flame straight onto Jimmy. He quickly fought to contain the fire to keep it from escaping to the wooden privacy fence in his yard. He had turned from Grill-man to firefighter. He walked into the house and my daughter said she gasped when she saw him. His eye brows and arm hair were gone. His face was covered in soot and from the way it was described to me; he was now a potential burn victim. Thank goodness he wasn't seriously injured. Everyone can now laugh but at the moment, it was serious. He won't even think of grilling now. Jimmy put the grill in the alley behind his house for the garbage guys to pick up. He has not grilled since. He goes out for steaks. The point is that sometimes, even with the best planning and equipment; unforeseen events can alter the desired outcome. Could Jimmy have predicted what happened, maybe, but he grew up where wind was not an issue and his point of reference told him how to grill, it didn't prepare him for how to grill in Kansas. What is the famous proverbial statement, "the best laid plans of mice and men, oft go awry"?   It's used to explain the futility of making detailed plans when your ability to fully or even partially execute the plan is uncertain. Sometimes, like when Jimmy turned from Grill-man into Fireman, you as the salesperson may have to turn from salesperson to Fireman. Your future business with that client may hang in the balance. You may have fires to put out that catch you off guard. Don't panic, act. Develop an action contingency plan that you will put in place when the sale doesn't work out the way you intended. Don't ignore the customers concerns, they are genuine. Own up to the product failure, your failure or the event failure. Take responsibility for the error and put your contingency plan into action. Be swift. Don't delay acting. Don't minimize the impact on the customer. There will be time to laugh about it in the future but now is not the time. Make it right and let the customer know that you will make it right. Do everything in your power to correct the situation but for yourself, remember, we all make mistakes; products don't always perform the way we think they will and sometimes it will be a disaster of our own making. Make good decisions seems an over simplification because what does that mean, does it imply that I wasn't making good decisions when I sold the product? Mistakes happen. I quite often am the reason they put erasers on the end of pencils and oops is not a bad four-letter word. Sometimes it's the way we learn.

Anyone up for a cookout?

Nothing Sells Itself

I am nine years old and sitting in the doctor's office with a raging case of poison ivy. I was covered from head to toe in a pink dried lotion that I couldn't even pronounce. It was late May and school had just let out for the summer. I had gone swimming in the nearby lake and the doctor was explaining to my mother that the oil from the poison ivy plant must have been on top of the water, like floating pollen, and guess what, I am allergic. I got a shot, more bitter tasting medicine and more lotion to spread all over me. This one was white. As I was sitting in the office trying not to scratch, I picked up a comic book but I couldn't concentrate on the comics so I began flipping through the pages until I got to the back. The ad jumped out at me like a bee to an open soft drink can. There it was; the sweetest ride a kid had ever seen. A shiny red dream of a ride and it could be mine if I sold Burpee seeds. The ad told me how great it would be to receive this wonder ride of a bicycle. I daydreamed and could see myself jumping over hills and riding to the store to get a coke. No more walking to the store, I was going to ride in style. I was hooked and all I had to do was sell seeds. Count me in. I could sell, I already had experience talking sweet old ladies out of vanilla cookies and the fact that I had not been that successful with my best friend Joel in getting extra cookies, didn't seem to bother me. I was zeroed in on that bike. I had sold my local homemade newspaper that I wrote (only one issue ever typed). It takes a lot of work to type so that business didn't last but one issue, our neighbor kindly bought the only copy but I was not deterred. I tore the ad out and started dreaming. I wrote the Burpee seed company a letter and sent it along with my $1 to the address on the ad. I had been collecting coke bottles along the road that led to the grocery store for some time and turned them in for five cents apiece. I sent this hard earned money to them and waited for the details of how many packs of seeds I needed to sell to get the bike. I got the seed packets back from Burpee and the deal was this. Sell 1,500 cartons of ten packs and the bike would be mine. A piece of cake I thought, my mom would by some, and the neighbors would buy the rest. Okay, maybe I was naive but as a kid I didn't know that it was a large number, all I could see was the bicycle. I just didn't make the connection about how daunting of a task it would be; I just thought "I can do this". I started my sales campaign and soon learned that it would be an astronomical amount of seed packs to sell. I guess I had worn out the neighbors with the other junk I had tried to sell. I didn't sell enough at five cents each to even recoup my initial investment before I ran out of seeds.

Cute will only get you so far in sales.

I would have to order more seeds, wait for them to arrive and then find new customers. Add to this the fact that my mother forbid me going to people we didn't know and it is an understatement to say my enthusiasm waned, but I had learned something. Nothing sells itself, it takes hard work. The point of this story is two-fold. One, that a career in sales takes hard work and training. Two, don't go swimming in May when the pollen is on top of the water if you are allergic to poison ivy.

"No" Humor

My Wife is a smart aleck. She is witty and always uses humor to get her points across. We jokingly say she has talented turrets syndrome. I mean no offense to anyone with the disability, I am trying to make a point of her instantaneous quick wit. She is probably one of the smartest people I know and I admire her quick wit. I wish I had it. She has passed this trait onto my daughters. They are both witty. I may be the king of my castle but I am surrounded by comic jesters. I don't stand a chance. My best comeback is a pathetic "oh yeah?". My youngest daughter works in a highly technical field in a highly regulated industry. She is an expert in the regulatory part of the business. She was attending a meeting of thirty or so managers and executives at the company she works for about a new rule that had been handed down by a regulator. The ongoing topic of the meeting was the expense and time that the new rule would add to their business costs and how that was going to impact the ongoing profitability of the business. The additional costs were burdensome. There was a faction of management that favored an approach that would push back on the regulator against what the executives and managers saw as an overreach of the regulators powers. They felt a concerted push back was the correct course. My daughter had already given her opinion that clarifying the new rules with the regulator should be the approach the company should pursue; she was not so much concerned about the cost of implementation of the new rules, just the compliance end of the equation. For her, the new rules were the rules of the game and if you wanted to play, you had to follow the new rules. The "how to comply" with the new regulator concerns were a better course in her mind than the course pushing back and fighting windmills. The discussions continued and as meeting often do, went on and on. It finally reached a point with her that her sarcastic wit kicked in. The group that insisted in pushing back on what management saw as unfair regulator edicts and demands had the upper hand. When the meeting got around to her group a second time, they asked if she had any further constructive input to add, she busted out in song and sang out a verse from Buddy Holly's hit song "I fought the law and the law won". The room erupted in laughter but her point was made. You may not like the regulations that come down from government regulators but you have to operate within them. She would not give any support for pushing back against a regulator beyond what had already been decided. Clarifying the new rule was okay but she was getting tired of the he discussion and the long meeting that companies slip into, so the decision for her was easy. She didn't see any need to have a thirty person meeting on a rule that had already been handed down. Delivering her point with humor defused a hotly debated point and brought the meeting to an abrupt end, something she often does in her mother's way, a funny and witty conclusion. Sometimes you have to say "no" to a customer, boss or potential client but you can avoid the "kill the messenger" effect that can tarnish or even destroy the sale by finding the humor in the situation that both you and your customer would understand. Make the "no" more palatable. Like Mary Poppins said" a spoonful of sugar helps the medicine go down" and humor is the sugar. While the no is still present and in effect, it will be easier to accept and understand by the customer. The sale can continue on to a successful conclusion and won't be derailed by a "no". Remember "no humor".

Family Court

My oldest daughter wants to take the youngest to family court. Family court has a judge, usually me, a juror, usually my wife, a defendant and a plaintiff. Everyone gets to tell their side of the story and then a vote occurs to decide the outcome. Sometimes punishment is muted out, like the time I lost in family court on where we were going to go on a weekend vacation. I had promised the water park but delivered on my wife's request to go to the outlet mall instead. My daughters saw the injustice and I had to pay big time on that one, I had to buy each of them a new outfit, including the judge, it was no coincidence that my wife was the judge on that case . Family court is also corrupt. Sometimes the defendant and plaintiff will conspire against me and even though I am the judge, I will lose the vote and have to abide by the courts decision on shopping. I hate to shop. It's our family's way of handling non-parental issues like the contract that has just come up because my oldest has just told my youngest to clean her room. She says the youngest has to because she signed a contract. The youngest is crying, she doesn't want to clean her sister's room and as a side note, she doesn't like cleaning her own room, it is a disaster. My wife really stresses out about how messy my youngest's room is, but I tell her not to worry about it unless it comes out into the hall. My wife huffs and doesn't like it. The youngest runs to her mother for help in this family dispute. The oldest wants to take the youngest to family court to enforce her contract saying that she had the youngest sign this agreement in exchange for helping her with her abc's. The oldest has manipulated the youngest by handing the younger one a piece of paper and saying "sign this". The "it", is a statement that the youngest will clean the oldest ones room forever. The youngest signed because she looked up to the oldest and trusted her. If the oldest told her to do something then the youngest did it. She is an innocent loving and trusting soul and the older one took advantage of that innocence to create a situation where the oldest could manipulate for her own benefit. This is a classic family court issue and court is now in session. My wife is the judge on this one and she issues a summary judgement in favor of the youngest by telling the oldest that the contact isn't enforceable because it wasn't notarized. Case dismissed. We need to have a family ethics lesson. Manipulation without profit for both is wrong. Knowing but doing it anyway is not what we do as people. It is okay to manipulate for profit where both the buyer and seller, in this case, my youngest and oldest, both benefit with full knowledge of what they are agreeing to. Manipulation is permitted but when only one understands the consequences and the other has gotten most if not all the benefit, well it won't stand up to scrutiny in family court. Being able to get someone to do something through nefarious methods is also not allowed. We have rules of behavior and we all follow them. The ability to convince others but not really understanding how you know how you do it, is sometimes called unconscious competence. The ability to recognize the moment someone is ready to purchase and taking advantage of that moment is skill. It's like driving a nail into a board. Instinctively you know that if you keep the head of the hammer centered on the nail and hit the nail on either the top left or the top right, you can direct the nail, and sometimes correct for the tendency of the nail to bend. Being able to control the bend and direction of the nail, helps drive home the point. In sales it's about using these techniques so fluidly and so routinely, they become ingrained into your everyday behavior and you recognize them when others use them, expertly or not. Being so skilled that you don't do it for cheap manipulation or for fun, but only for profit, and by profit I mean to help the customer get what they want and need. You have the skills and you also have ethics. You are a pro. You are not a con man out to cheat anyone and you aren't in sales just for a quick buck, but truly endeavor to help others get what they want and need; and in the process, gratefully accept the financial rewards that accompany a job well done.

Tidbit #4   Manipulation vs. Selling

My brother-in-law Rocky is telling his four-year-old granddaughter Aubrey that when "Nanna" goes to the store, they will play a game of picking up rocks and throwing them out of the yard; Then we will wash grandpa's truck. Oh, it will be fun. Aubrey quickly replies in her sweetest tone, "grandpa, you will just have to play by yourself". Even a four-year-old can spot manipulation.

Senior Discount

My wife is a champion at couponing. I conservatively estimate that she saves us ten to fifteen percent on our purchasing budget yearly by couponing or knowing which restaurant has what special on which days. She routinely has me ask the wait server for a senior discount and she even brags to the other women at her monthly card game that "my man can get the senior discount". I am a senior citizen, she is not. On Sundays you can catch her cutting out coupons from the Sunday newspaper and going through her coupon folder getting rid of the expired ones we haven't used. You may laugh but it adds up to about five thousand dollars a year based on our average spending of about three thousand dollars a month. She saves on everything. On one occasion we were visiting one of our daughters that lives in Houston and were discussing the savings my daughter had just gotten off a purse she was buying from the coupon my wife had just given to her. My wife was expounding on the benefits of couponing as we pulled into the restaurant after a long day of shopping. We had stopped at an upscale Italian restaurant that we have eaten at in the past and she proudly said "I think I have a coupon for this place" and grabbed her coupon folder from the side door of the car where she keeps it. We hadn't planned on eating at this restaurant and since we don't even have this restaurant chain in our state, I seriously doubted she had a coupon, and I said so. We often tease her about her coupon skills, but we love the savings. She countered saying that she thought she did and I said adamantly and confidently that I would kiss her behind if she had one. I thought it was a sure bet. Well let's just say pucker up butter cup, she had one. A few months later we were grocery shopping and one of the items they had in their store sale paper was on special, but they didn't have it on the shelf. My wife asked me to go to the customer service desk and ask for a rain check coupon so that we could use it in the future when they got the product back on the shelf. As I was doing this my wife checked out. She placed her groceries on the counter and after everything was rung up, she headed out to the car. I finished getting the rain check and caught up to her but noticed she seemed to be in a different mood than what she was in the store. I put the groceries in the back of the car, climbed in the front seat and my wife turned to me and in a growl, said "do I look like a senior to you". I'm no dummy, I have been married for forty years, I said no? You look as young as ever. She went on to explain that the clerk that checked her out "had asked, if she wanted her senior discount", she "said she wanted to just slap him". She then went on to tell me it was our niece's fault for not coloring her hair before our trip down to Houston. She stated that respecting people was a basic job criteria for sales clerks and he was totally rude to her. She went on for a good two minutes telling me how rude that young man was. I knew I was on shaky ground but I asked my wife, "how old are you, aren't you a senior now", she had just had a birthday; she said yes but how dare the clerk say such a thing.

If you are cold calling on a business and the first person you meet is a woman, don't ask is she is the secretary; if she is the owner, you will have created a problem for yourself for no reason. If she is the manager, purchasing buyer, or other important contact person you need to speak to in order to start the sales process, you will have just created a major faux-pax that you may not recover from. Don't assume gender or sexual preference, because if you are wrong and you probably will be, you will be a pariah forever and the sale will never have the chance to get off the ground. The point is, stay cognizant to gender sensibilities and treat everyone you meet with the respect you would give someone of your own gender. A gentle and firm, but not crushing handshake, will be interpreted as respect. Not getting their name correct will be regarded as disrespect or indifference, and depending on how you handle the introductions, directly influence the direction of the sale. Trying not to offend sounds obvious but if you ask whether the woman you just met is pregnant, and she is not and simply happens to be overweight, you will have created a chasm you won't be able to go back across. If you think she is a senior citizen entitled to your senior discount simply because you see she has gray hair, and she is not, you will not be forgiven. If you are simply talking to fill a silence while you are waiting to see whoever you are here to see, you will risk offending the very busy person you are interrupting. Unfortunately, there are multiple ways of offending people but doing so because of our own insensitiveness' is at the top of the oh-oh, my bad list. It may not be lethal to your sale but it won't move it forward either. Pre-planned talk is productive if it includes asking questions you don't know the answer to and the information you gain is useful to moving the sale but personal interactions are complicated and what seems like a minor thing can become a major roadblock to the sale of your own creation. I don't mean you should walk around on egg shells but it is important to be more than self-aware but socially and gender aware. It creates customer service experiences that affect not only this sale but all future sales. If it's your business, and your livelihood depends on it, how do you want your customers to be treated? People think customer service has gone the way of full service gas stations where they used to run out and pump your gas but people pay for self-service, they become repeat buyers with good assisted self-service. My wife to this day, does not like going to that grocery store; except on senior discount day. She likes her discount and won't let her vanity interfere with her goal of saving money but she doesn't like shopping there. We only go on senior day and only buy the specials. We go to a different big box retailer for other things, so the store is not getting the maximum business from her that they could have if the sales clerks were trained better. Don't laugh at sensitivity training. It can pay off in thousands of dollars in additional business if you are smart enough to recognize what the amateurs don't. My wife saves us about five grand a year with couponing on thirty-six thousand dollars' worth of sales; I often wonder how many sales dollars the store is missing out on because of her shopping experience?

Only One Can Speak

My wife brought home a package of grocery stores generic crème filled vanilla cookies, you know the ones, the family pack of 24 cookies per package, made to look like the name brand cookies but not a hint of chocolate anywhere to be found. She served them with lemonade. Real gourmet desert stuff. Suddenly a memory of my childhood came rushing back to when I was a child. As children we would go to vacation bible school and that's what they would serve us for a mid-morning snack, two vanilla crème cookies and a Dixie paper cup half full of lemonade. It was half full because they didn't want you spilling it all over the church floor. Wow, was it good. So good in fact that I would try to get an extra cookie to make it three. My best friend Joel was right there with me and I'm convinced that had Joel kept quiet when I asked for the third cookie, we would have succeeded but Joel, fearing he was being left out, kept interrupting saying "me to, me to". It's funny how a vanilla cookie can trigger a memory that has lasted a long time. I hadn't started in my soon to be short lived Burpee seed sales career yet but I learned that if Joel had been quiet when I asked the closing question, "can I have an extra", we would have feasted on extra vanilla cookies every morning of the week. I was a cute kid and hard to say no to. My point is this; when you ask a closing question, shut up. Don't interrupt. Don't talk because the first person to speak, whether it is the salesperson or the customer will determine the direction of the sale. If the customer speaks, it will be to continue the sales process or the customer will present an opportunity objection. The customer will be accepting the salespersons direction and finish the sale or decline with an objection. If the salesperson speaks or has someone with them that speaks, the sale will be directed away from the close and the customers focus will have been redirected. You may think the cookie was a cheap lesson, it wasn't. For a kid wanting to increase his cookie rewards it was a lesson in sales and a lesson that has stuck for all these years. Later in my career as a professional sales person I would have mangers that would want to ride along with me and go into the sale. Before going into see the customer I would explain the rule, only one person speaks. On one occasion we were calling on a customer to sell an antidote for patients that experienced a certain type of medication toxicity. There were several competitors in the marketplace. It was a large hospital and back then, salespeople could negotiate hospital contracts. I used an assumptive close with the customer by asking the customer what their hospitals legal address was as I handed the customer the sales agreement. The way it works is this. As the salesperson, you assume the customer is buying and hand the paperwork to the customer along with a pen, if they accept the paperwork and begin filling out the form, the sale is complete as long as no one speaks. You simply ask them to fill it in and point with a pen for where they are to begin. The manager didn't understand what an assumptive close was and felt the need to say something else because he did not understand the purpose of the rule, only one person speaks. He spoke to my customer when I handed the form to the customer. I'm sure he thought he was adding to the reasons to buy but what he really did was cause a misdirection of the sale process into areas that we were not going to compete in and that I had difficulty recovering from. I explained the shut up-don't interrupt concept to the manager once we had left and I reminded him that only one salesperson can speak, they can speak as the salesperson or I can, but not both. As an adult sale professional I was no longer talking about cookies, I was talking about my bonus.

Shut Up

In the social sciences, silence is the greatest pressure on earth. Our nature is to abhor a quiet vacuum, so we fill it with uh's, um's and other place holders that have no definition or purpose other than to fill the silence void with sound. Some people do it so much it can be very distracting in following their conversation. We feel the need to fill the quiet with sound. Try this experiment. Look into the eyes of your spouse and don't say anything but be sure to maintain eye contact. Wait for as long as it takes for your spouse to say something. Count the seconds in your head, one Mississippi, two Mississippi' and so on until the silence forces your spouse to say something. How long did it take? Two seconds, three? What you will find is that the silence between you will be cracked by your spouse telling you that they love you or questioning your reasons for the silence with the question "what?" Now try it with a stranger by asking a question. When you are greeted with the standard "hi, how are you today", answer by asking the identical question back to them but shut up, don't move, don't say anything and maintain eye contact. How long did it take to get an answer, a couple of seconds probably but no more. Was it awkward? Now try it in a sales situation. When you ask the customer to buy, shut up, maintain eye contact and do not move. Did it take very long to get an answer? Did it seem like a long time to get the answer? In reality it probably took the same amount of time to get an answer but it may have felt like minutes. Depending on the financial commitment you are asking for, it may feel like hours but don't move, don't speak and maintain eye contact. You will find that the customer will feel the pressure to respond to your question. The pressure will be so great that the customer will either buy or offer up an objection, but either way the sale will move forward. In nature, pressure can turn a piece of coal into a diamond and in sales the pressure of silence can turn an average salesperson into a shining star, but beware, the first person to speak will determine if the result will be a treasured gem or just another rock.

I Missed It

It is a beautiful, but hot July afternoon in Arkansas. Not a cloud in the crystal blue sky. It hasn't rained for weeks and the sun bearing down on me this Saturday seems relentless. What little shade from the dugout where the players are sitting has already been claimed by the other player's parents and the rest of us are sitting in the sun. The lesson here is to get to the ballpark early if you want a seat in the shadow of the dugout. I should have brought an umbrella. The ground is bare of grass and even the weeds have gone into hiding waiting on a rain. The dirt is a fine powder kicked up by the slightest breeze into a swirling dust tornado that cuts through the chain link fence and sends the crowd of parents reaching for their soft drinks to wash it down. My aluminum lawn chair is reflecting the heat from the sun like it's my own personal hot plate. I'm cooking here and the sweat is dripping from me like the badly missed rain. The crowd of proud is sitting on the edge of their seats, yelling instructions to the players who give up glances of irritation that they have been singled out by their moms or dads about being heads up. First batter up and it is a single to put the runner on first. Second batter hits to right field and the runner advances to second. Two on base. You can smell the dust in the air as the runner from second steals third by sliding into base and the runner on first also steals an advance. The next batter bunts and makes it to first. The bases are loaded and the other team has their players leading off, ready to steal home. This is strategy. It is preplanned by a coach that knows what he is doing. It's a routine tactic from teams that travel. Traveling teams don't play a local circuit, they play tournaments and they play to win. They have real coaches, not parent coaches like us and they intend to show no mercy. They place hit, steal bases and squash teams underfoot like so much fodder. They are well funded by their sponsors; a car dealership or an air conditioning company, I don't remember which, from another part of the state and rumors are that they even have their own team bus. They take girls softball very seriously. Their uniforms and equipment are the best while ours are t-shirts and shorts that each parent has put together and our equipment is whatever the parent can provide. One player on our team has so many logos on their outfit I jokingly call her check mark when I see her. Hat, shoes, shorts, socks and shirt, all have the logo. We are lucky this year, we have a sponsor and the girls have matching shirts that the local used car dealer has provided. Some of the iron on letters aren't ironed on all that well and are coming off but hey, we have uniforms. It's interesting the branding that occurs at the ball park and I have an idle thought about how much I could make selling branded team outfits to the parents. We could all be checkmarks. The thought passes and I'm back in the game. The visiting team plays every weekend during the season and their season lasts until the all teams have been vanquished in a tri state area. They go to district, regional and national tournaments. To say they play is an inaccuracy; they put on a well-practiced and orchestrated performance. We are about to be slaughtered. I am sweating profusely and dying of thirst. The sun keeps bearing down and I realize that we are way out of our league with this team. Someone has brought a stand up canopy with the poles and I get up to help put it together. I am not one to be indifferent to someone else's need of assistance, especially if I can also benefit from the shade that is being erected. I am holding one of the corners of the canopy and the pole while the parent is attaching the rope and anchor to the ground. Bases loaded, next batter hits a sacrifice fly to center field and third base tags up to steal home. Center field catches the fly ball and throws the ball to home plate where my daughter is crouched with her catcher's mask off ready for the play. The runner is just a moment behind the throw. She catches the ball, sweeps with the glove to her left in a perfectly executed single motion of poetry and tags the runner; she then leaps to her feet and throws to second base catching the runner coming from first before they reach the bag. Triple play; and, I MISSED IT! The play lasted just seconds. The parent crowd is going crazy and the game has erupted into yelling, clapping and screaming; We may be going to be beaten but not without a fight. There I am standing with my back to the game holding a pole. The runner had tried to escape the sweep of the glove but my daughter had been practicing for this moment for weeks in our back yard and performed it in a well-coordinated ballet of motion. A play of the week moment that had it been recorded on video, would be an example of perfect timing and execution; and I missed the whole thing for taking my eye off the game for my own benefit for one second. A once in a lifetime play, she won't be twelve for long. Parents are yelling, "did you see that?! No I didn't I think and it sucks. It was a tremendous play and was so great they would talk about it for the rest of the season. So great, that when the next runner came to third, the opposing coach motioned for the runner to stay on base and not to challenge this catcher with a run. The point of this story is don't take your eye off the sale for even a moment. Be there the instant the customer gives you a buying signal and be focused in the moment. When you have the opportunity to sweep the sale to a close, you'll be ready. What a great game selling is, don't miss it.

Best wishes and Good Selling